Jpr **POETRY**
Th Se

First Words

POETRY BY JOYCE SUTPHEN

Straight Out of View (1995)
Coming Back to the Body (2000)
Naming the Stars (2004)
Fourteen Sonnets (2005)

Joyce Sutphen

First Words

POEMS

Red Dragonfly Press ❧ Minnesota ❧ 2010

ISBN 978-1-890193-91-1
978-1-890193-92-8 (case bound)

Library of Congress Control Number: 2009940000

Special thanks to Connie Wanek, Tim Nolan, and others for careful and
insightful comments on the manuscript in progress; thanks also to the
Anderson Center in Red Wing, Minnesota, for a residency where some
of these poems were written, and many thanks to colleagues at Gustavus
Adolphus College for their ongoing encouragement. As always, I am
grateful to my family for their support and inspiration.

Support for this title was provided by the Tides Foundation.

See back of book for publication acknowledgments.

Cover images: Rassier Family photographs;
farm house photograph by Joyce Sutphen.

Typeset in Minion, a digital type designed by Robert Slimbach.

Printed in the United States of America
on 30% recycled stock
by Thomson-Shore, a worker owned company

Published by Red Dragonfly Press
press-in-residence at the Anderson Center
P. O. Box 406
Red Wing, MN 55066

For more information and additional titles visit our website
www.reddragonflypress.org

Contents

For my parents,

Bob & Rita Rassier

How You Learn

You don't need new words
or even new ways of putting

one word next to another.
No, you simply need to be

touched by the god who
has you tell what was not

in your mind. You just need
to let it come the way it will

as it leaps across the land,
skipping the way you usually

try to build a fire, teaching
you how to drive through

the dark. You don't need to
prepare except that you

already have in all the
lost pages and the sounds

that dissolved on your tongue.
At that moment, you gather

up the years like a shawl
and wrap yourself in them,

one corner touching another.
Everything you have done

is suddenly useful, and it turns
out there's a pattern after all.

Now I see the secret of making the best person: it is to grow in the open air and sleep with the earth.

—Walt Whitman

In the Family

My job was to lead the way,
to be an example,
to succeed first, fail first,
to leave and return.

No one could show me
where to go or what to do—
it was my job to figure that out.
I was the oldest, the first-born.

I didn't understand why
I had to do this. None of them
cared to follow me—they
weren't even watching.

After a while I came upon
a plan: I did everything
wrong; I found every
dead-end on the map.

Soon word got out:
whatever you do, don't
do what your sister did.
I was the warning now.

Like a signpost in County Clare,
pointing in all directions at once,
I would be the road not to take.
That much I could say for sure.

The Largest Room of My Childhood

My other name would be
far away or gone to the moon.
I would be leaves falling—
the sky at sunset.

My heart would be neat
as a clock, or a hat
on its hook—I would be nothing
but flat horizon,

or something that would not float,
a stone dropping
through waters, rain—
cloud to ground.

How long would I remain
at the bottom of the lake?
I might stay there
forever.

The Before I Was Born Blues

I wasn't born the year she sang that song,
but I miss it anyway. I miss the
clarinet that starts it out; I miss the
way the lady says he done her wrong.

I would've liked a red-feathered hat,
a tailored suit and high-heeled shoes, a pearl
necklace—a single strand—and leather gloves.
Nothing I wear will ever look like that.

There's something about the saxophone
and the piano slightly off the beat
that makes me imagine someone handsome
who's just about to fall in love with me,

and god, I wish I knew what happens when
he turns and . . . too bad—I wasn't born then.

All the Colors

My great-grandparents
were sepia—always

wedding clothes, seldom smiling—
they gazed from their bronze world

into the black and white era
of my grandparents,

who sometimes let themselves
be caught in their Sunday best,

still carefully arranged—
almost breaking into smile

when my parents arrived,
laughing, happy as movie stars—

they lifted me up to the camera—
all the colors, coming into view.

The Body I Once Lived In

The body I once lived in was smaller.
It stood at the top of the stairs and waved
good-night; it wore pajamas that had feet.

That body could swing on ropes in the hay barn
and run alongside wagons in the field.
That one loved to eat pancakes and sausages.

The body I once lived in sucked her thumb
and had nightmares about rattlesnakes and pigs.
Next day, the rooster crowed; the sun came up

and the body I once lived in walked out
over the dewy grass to let the cows
into the barn, stood in the aisle watching

until a head was in each place, then closed
the stanchions one by one and brought the milkers
in. That body did not look in mirrors.

That one never wore shoes in summer,
except on Sundays, only took a bath
on Saturdays, wore whatever clothes fit.

Krinkletop Cookies

What was nice about that recipe
was that it didn't require eggs
and that it was something my mother's

mother's grandmother made. "Krinkletops,"
we called them, close to what my great-great-
grandmother called them in the Old World.

I always measured the sugar first
(white, scooped from the bin),
then added lard from the crock

and dark molasses poured out
in a mahogany ribbon. Then flour,
sifted with ginger, cloves,

cinnamon, and soda to make
a sweet and spicy smell, which was
another nice thing about that recipe—

that and the pleasure of rolling
dough into balls (dipped in sugar
and pressed down on the cookie sheet)

and seeing the righteous hills
rise up and collapse into rows
of cracked and krinkled sugar deserts.

My Legendary Father

Here are some other things he could do: he
could weld old water pipes into a swing;
he could build a mountain out of snow; he

could lay a field of hay flat, then twist it
into long green ribbons and pack it up
into bales for winter; he could squirt a

stream of milk into a kitten's open
"meow"; he could carry four roosters at
once, all of them swinging upside down, their

yellow feet gathered like kindling in his
big hands; he could ride a horse bareback, no
bridle, and on Sundays he could be our

eternal pitcher, sending one perfect
strike after another over home-plate.

Afternoon Concerto

It opens with the wind, gusting.
The birds enter gradually,

as if on cue: blackbirds
and grackles, crows

puncturing the distant skies,
starlings layered into

the drone of airplane overhead.
A bird I've only just learned

to identify as a sora sings, almost
drowned out by another airplane

and the trucks on the highway
behind the line of trees. The wind

crescendos, beating its green drums
until a branch snaps and falls.

Red-winged blackbirds enter
with a crazy song, like

cracked bells chiming. Finally,
the sweet sound of the lawnmower

across the afternoon, engine and
blade turning leaves into grass.

Rhubarb

I can tell you nothing
about its relatives
or the uses it had
in China.

For us, it simply grew
at the end of the garden—
a ruby-red wand
for the sugar bin.

My mother chopped it into pieces
and made pies, cakes and sauces.
She gave it in armfuls
to her friends.

Just last week, I watched her bend
and pull out a stalk with both
hands, then pass it—like a
torch—on to me.

Birds of Stearns County

The first were barn swallows, gliding
through an open door
to reach their mud nests in the rafters,

and after that crows, black on the white
branches in the cow yard,
dour as parish priests,

then pigeons in the haybarn,
plump silhouettes
in the high window,

robins under the apple trees,
heads bent over red breasts,
worrying for worms,

the lark, down in the meadow,
swaying on a reed
beyond the wild iris,

and a hawk, always circling,
waiting for a ripple
in the grass.

The Kingdom of Summer

In my mother's cellar there were
realms of golden apple, rooms
of purple beet, hallways of green bean
leading to windows of
strawberry and grape.

In her cellar there were
cider seas and
pumpkin shores,
mountains of tomatoes
pickle trees.

When I walked down the steps
and pulled on the light,
I saw where she kept the
Kingdom of Summer.

Canning

It's what she does and what her mother did.
It's what I'd do if I were anything
like her mother's mother—or if the times
demanded that I work in my garden,
planting rows of beans and carrots, weeding
the pickles and potatoes, picking worms
off the cabbages.

                          Today she's canning
tomatoes, which means there are baskets
of red Jubilees waiting on the porch
and she's been in the cellar looking for jars.
There's a box of lids and a heap of gold
rings on the counter.   She gets the spices
out; she revs the engine of the old stove.

Now I declare her Master of Preserves!
I say that if there were degrees in canning
she would be *summa cum laude*—God knows
she's spent as many hours at the sink peeling
the skins off hot tomatoes as I have
bent over a difficult text. I see
her at the window, filling up the jar,
packing a glass suitcase for the winter.

The Aunts

I like it when they get together
and talk in voices that sound
like apple trees and grape vines,

and some of them wear hats
and go to Arizona in the winter,
and they all like to play cards.

They will always be the ones
who say "It is time to go now,"
even as we linger at the door;

or stand by the waiting cars, they
remember someone—an uncle we
never knew—and sigh, all

of them together, like wind
in the oak trees behind the farm
where they grew up—a place

I remember—especially
the hen house and the soft
clucking that filled the sunlit yard.

Mango Poem

It's because of words that I want to eat
a mango, that I want to be someplace

where they grow mangoes in season and where
I can hear the mango skin rip away

from the fruity flesh, where I can watch the
surface lift off the golden mango globe.

There are no mangoes in Minnesota
like the mangoes of Indonesia,

and in my family no recipe
that describes how to make a sauce out of

mango, tamarind and lemongrass; there's
no one to tell me how the mango bud

will make my voice sweet and no one to hear
all the beautiful words for the mango.

My Luck

When I was five, my father,
who loved me, ran me over
with a medium-sized farm tractor.

I was lucky though; I tripped
and slipped into a small depression,
which caused the wheels to tread

lightly on my leg, which had already
been broken (when I was three)
by a big dog, who liked to play rough,

and when I was nine, I fell
from the second-floor balcony
onto the cement by the back steps,

and as I went down I saw my life go by
and thought: "This is exactly how
Wiley Coyote feels, every time!"

Luckily, I mostly landed on my feet,
and only had to go on crutches
for a few months in the fifth grade—

and shortly after that, my father,
against his better judgment,
bought the horse I'd wanted for so long.

All the rest of my luck has to do
with highways and ice—things that
could have happened, but didn't.

Zucchini Bread

All of the recipes were a form
of defense—a highly
developed system of
culinary martial arts
designed to chop, shred, slice
and disintegrate
the zucchini,

which proliferates at
an astounding rate so
that it appears
like a sly green jack-in-the-box
under every wide leaf
and fills the baskets and covers
the kitchen counters until
the conscientious
and careful cook can do
nothing but bake and
bake.

One summer we ate
even the flowers, dipped
in batter and deep-fried
to a golden crisp.
Covering yours
in maple syrup, you said
"not bad"—just
like you said
the bread
didn't taste at all
like zucchini.

Counting to a Hundred

I don't know why I did it—only that
I resorted to the comfort of counting
to a hundred as I sat among the ferns

in the sun-porch of Miss Marie T. Kamer's
parents' home after lessons on the piano
(seventy-five cents for one half-hour

in one of John Thompson's red books).
I was waiting for my mother to come
and rescue me from that tiny house

under the gigantic elm trees—my mother,
who wanted to stretch out that half-hour, while
Marie shrank it down to the metronome's

minute and then retreated to another
part of the house, where her ancient parents
also waited, like specters, for me to leave.

I knew my mother found us hard to bear,
but I did not think she would leave
me there in the darkened porch and beyond

to the silent room where the piano
was closed and the statue of a gold horse
with a clock in its stomach tick-tocked from

the mantle and dolls with dresses made out
of milk filters and pipe cleaners were
propped on the plastic-covered furniture.

I wanted to go home to our kitchen
and the wood-fire stove, to my brothers
playing with Tonka trucks in their pajamas.

I would even go peacefully to bed and
promise not to read under the covers, if only
she'd come . . . before I counted to a hundred.

Hanging Wash

The first load was all sheets, pillowcases,
dish towels, white handkerchiefs,
and underwear. I went out of the screen door

with the heavy wicker basket and carried it
up the hill to the lilacs and the granary,
my feet bare in the wet grass.

The empty wash lines dangled against the sky.
One cloud lifted away I dropped
the basket under the first line and went

to get the canvas bag of clothespins.
After that I was all arms stretching laundry
from point to point, calculating the distance

sheet by sheet, already imagining the baskets
filled with t-shirts, pajamas, jeans,
long gray socks and red bandanas.

All morning I went up and down the hill
as the wind filled and fluttered the wash
on the line and dried the grass beneath my feet.

In the woods beyond the fence posts,
the cows went by—a fleet of
black and white ships setting sail.

Jiffy Mazola Cake

The recipe was in my mother's
perfect handwriting, each letter looking
exactly like the ones in our copybook—

the right height to the t, the little hills
of the m's and the n's, the r—which always
reminded me of the stump of a tree.

The dry ingredients, on the left side
of the card, were joined together
with a sharp-nosed bracket:

sugar, flour, cocoa powder, baking soda,
salt. The bracket said sift until
a dusky mountain rises in the big bowl,

form a crater at the top of the mountain
and measure out the following ingredients
(another bracket): whole milk, vinegar,

and—of course—the gold Mazola oil,
which would float, briefly, like a jewel in
the souring milk and wash through

the cocoa-flour mountain like a tidal
wave. The next instructions were precise:
beat fifty strokes with a large spoon—do *not*

over-beat. Pour into pan which has been
greased and floured. Run knife through
the batter to prevent air bubbles; bake

at 350 until the cake springs back
when you press your finger (very lightly)
on the dark brown surface. Cool.

Polka Revival

And what if one day
everyone wants to oom-pah-pah-pah
and sing "Roll Out the Barrel"?

What if "In Heaven There is No Beer"
replaces the National Anthem? What if large guys
with accordions take over MTV?

Just think: if polka music becomes the rage,
the fact that in your childhood the radio
was perpetually tuned to a station

that only played Whoopee John
and the Deutchmasters will be a legend
that impresses your grandchildren.

Tell us, they'll say, how they played polkas
between something called "The Livestock
Market" and "The Trading Post,"

and how you begged your parents to turn the dial
to Elvis, Buddy Holly, Duane Eddy, and Dion
(whoever *they* were)

and then tell us how they refused—
how they kept the polka going and danced
circles around the kitchen.

First Words

My father and mother must have said
many things, because I had to learn all
my first words from them—no television,

no day care—just a man and a woman
in the circle that makes a farm—
house and barn, shop and granary,

chicken coop, silos, machine shed
and corn crib. My grandparents had built
a house in town, but they came back

with their own words and their voices
slipped into the ones I was learning—
cow, chicken, dog, pig, and horse,

tractor, fences, rhubarb, please and
thank you. Lilacs. I must have listened to
the radio with its livestock reports

and polkas—and then on Sundays
there was Latin—*Introibo*
ad altare Dei, which I did not

understand, any more than I did
the milk machine pumping like
a heart to draw down the warm milk.

ॐ

The grower of trees, the gardener, the man born to farming,
whose hands reach into the ground and sprout,
to him the soil is a divine thing.

—Wendell Berry, "The Man Born to Farming"

Just For the Record

It wasn't like that. Don't imagine
my father in a feed cap, chewing
a stem of alfalfa, spitting occasionally.

No bib-overalls over bare shoulders,
no handkerchief around his neck.
Don't imagine he didn't shave every morning.

The buildings on his farm weren't
weathered gray; the lawns were always mowed.
Don't imagine a car in the weeds.

I tell you this because you have certain
ideas about me, about farmers
and their daughters.

You imagine him bumbling along, some
hayseed, when really, he wore his dark
suit as gracefully as Cary Grant.

The one thing you're right about
is that he worked too hard. You can't
imagine how early and how late.

Bringing in the Hay

There must have been a dozen other times
when we finished making hay just before

the skies opened, but I remember best
the time that I rode home on the wagon,

looking back at the bare hayfield, pointing
to the clouds gathered in the West (angry

thunderheads, forking streaks of lightning),
and saw the fingered tunnel descending.

Something was up in the sky, bellying
down over our fields, and I could see how

we looked from above: a man on a red
tractor pulling a wagon load of hay,

a girl sitting on the top bale calling
to the black and white dog that trailed behind.

The beast surveyed the scene, and then because
we were meant to live, moved on to the East.

We had the hay in the barn, and supper
was on the table when the rains came down.

On the 4th of July

Perhaps it only happened once
that we missed the cotton candy,

the bingo tent, the fishing pond,
and the pie room, because

(as everyone knows) you have
to make hay when the sun is shining,

and so we stayed home that 4th,
bringing in loads of hay,

while up at the celebration,
the town kids wandered under

striped tents, drinking cool bottles
of root beer, taking a spin

at the cake walk, waiting
for the fireworks to begin—

but now it's that 4th of July
I want—back at the farm again,

blue sky over the hayfield
and the red tractor and baler

swiveling along the green rows,
bales dropping at perfect intervals,

as if measuring out a happiness
we didn't even know we had.

Of Gravel and Clay

Sometimes the road wanted more gravel—
then we'd go down to the gravel pit

with a wagon made of wheels
and two-by-fours. My father slung

shovelfuls of sand into the wagon,
and I picked out the chunks of gold

that threaded through our land
like veins in a living body.

I liked how the clay held itself together—
unlike the fickle gravel that

would slip out from between the boards
to fill any rut in the road.

Picking Rocks

The object was to remove objects
from the field. We did this every

year, and every year the rocks came
back again in Spring, as if the sky

was a big blue magnet, drawing
them up through the tangled roots

of last year's crop, or spilling them
from above, like the time my mother

dropped a jar of buttons on the floor.
We stumbled as we gathered, grumbled

a little, half-working, half-dreaming
through the wind-swept April day,

our eyes scanning the trees for green,
checking the slough for pussywillows

to bring to school—the one evidence
of our rural life the nuns always liked.

My Dog Pal

Once, in the yellow glow of the hay barn,
my father and I met a stray, and that dog
stayed and lived with us a while.

I named him "Pal" because he was friendly
and reminded me of a storybook dog.
Even now I can see him sitting

at my feet, his head tipped slightly to one
side, his shoulders squared back against
the passing of another boring day.

Thin and houndy, he was made for wilder
things than fetching sticks and shaking hands with
six-year olds. I think he was a hobo dog,

and one day he was gone, without
a backwards glace; his house, his dish, his supper
bone—nothing there to tie him down.

Asking My Father About the Horses

When I ask him if he'd remember how
to harness a horse, he says, "After all
these years? No problem." So I ask does he
ever miss them. "Who?" he says, and I say
the horses. "Oh them." No, he was happy
when the tractors came. "A tractor kept on
going. With the horses, you had to stop
and rest. You couldn't push them, and horses
got sick and hot, and the flies bothered them."

Wasn't there anything you liked better
about the horses? "I liked their eyes, the
way they lifted their heads and whinnied when
I walked into the barn. I liked hearing
the land turning behind me as I plowed."

In the Time of Pitchforks

This was before bales, before the raked hay
slipped between the baler's teeth and came out
in heavy green packages tied with twine.

This was back in the time of pitchforks, when
tractors weren't much bigger than a team
of horses, when wagons were made of wood,

when the hay-loader—tall as a silver
giraffe—followed in back of the wagon
and the hay row climbed up like a salmon

and fell out of the blue sky down onto
the platform, where my father stood pitching
the hay—first to one side, then the other—

layering a green sea over the ropes
that would lift and swing it into the barn.

Breakfast

My father taught me how to eat breakfast
those mornings when it was my turn to help
him milk the cows. I loved rising up from

the darkness and coming quietly down
the stairs while the others were still sleeping.
I'd take a bowl from the cupboard, a spoon

from the drawer, and slip into the pantry
where he was already eating spoonfuls
of cornflakes covered with mashed strawberries

from our own strawberry fields forever.
Didn't talk much—except to mention how
good the strawberries tasted or the way

those clouds hung over the hay barn roof.
Simple—that's how we started up the day.

Harrow

I want to praise
the harrow,
first for its name,
which when I write it,

is like unto what it is,
and that (as I remember)
is a collection of iron points
held together by
a wide and wooden frame.

Nothing about
the harrow is harrowing—
leave that to the mower
or the combine.

The harrow comes
after the disk, which comes
after the plow. The plow
was yesterday; the harrow
is now.

For the harrow rides
over the field, it moves
like a stream over rock,
like rain on the roof.

For when the world
is turned inside
out, the harrow
slips it back into
its skin again.

The Small Fields

The small fields I once knew were not
joined to one another so that tractors

as big as my father's shop could roll
up and down the gentle hills without ever

turning a page, without coming to the end
of a line, without leaving a margin along

the fence posts of the lane to the meadow—
where cows, each one with a name,

went down—a black and white procession
in search of greener pastures—tails swishing,

their great heads swinging side to side, each
taking a turn to bellow at the sky,

while off in the distance, a small tractor
went back and forth between the rows of corn.

Threshing Machine

Fifty years later and at seventy miles
an hour I see a threshing machine on
a hill alongside a highway. Too small,

I think, because in my memory
a threshing machine is as big as a house
belching smoke, filling the air with the noise

of wheels and pulleys, the groan of engines
turning the crashing maelstrom at the heart
of the beast we served when the oats ripened.

The way I remember it, tractors and trucks
revolved like planets around the hub
of the universe, like acolytes to the god

of the harvest who consumed all,
whose hunger was swift and would never
be appeased until field by field the shocks

were lifted into the wagons and brought
in bundles to be flung to the thresher
where the oats were separated from the straw

in golden streams—such a delicate trick,
the parting of kernel and chaff, as in
the end of summer—the end of the world.

The Oat Binder

First, I had to explain an oat field
and how it is green, then gold—
waves of it, like wheat, but with
a different kind of head, and how the
oat binder cut down the ripened oats
with its sideways sharp teeth and let
it fall flat onto the canvas platform,
then carried it along under the wooden
wings turning like paddle wheels on
a river boat, gathered it into bundles,
and then—through some crafty sleight of
its mechanical hand—tied up the bundle
and dropped it back to the stubbled field.

Then I had to explain how we came
walking through the field to set the bundles
together like this: three pairs, head to head,
and one pulled over the top, like a hat
(we called this "shocking the oats"), and then
I had to tell about the threshing machine,
how it was as big as houses and how
it lumbered down the hill behind the county's
oldest tractor like a tamed behemoth,
and how its handlers—Harold and Elmer—
were missing parts of their arms and legs.

But I didn't tell about the wagons, the
pitchforks, and the tractor standing back,
attached to a long belt that turned wheels that
turned the wheels on the threshing machine,
and if you touched that belt it was like
touching fire, and I didn't say anything
about the pickup trucks waiting to receive
the oats and carry it back to the granaries.
But I did talk about the straw, as it fell
like Rapunzel's hair into a yellow heap,
but then I had to explain straw, how it

was beautifully flat and smooth (not stiff
and scratchy like hay, not something cows ate)
and how we shook it out under the cows
as they swished their tails in the warm barn,
while the snow gathered in drifts all around.

And I explained about the men in the
threshing crew and how they worked from
farm to farm, dawn to dusk, only stopping
at noon to wash their blackened hands
and devour plates filled with meat and mashed
potatoes, gravy, dressing, three kinds of
vegetables, stacks of bread with butter and
jam, pickles, applesauce, and then (of
course) pie and coffee. I suppose I mentioned
(again) how I helped in the fields until
I had to help in the kitchen and how
I hated being the girl who filled the
water glasses and served the pies, staying
behind to do the dishes before I could
go back to the fields, but it wasn't worth
complaining now to someone who never
saw an oat binder—or a threshing machine
or a horse in harness—and who couldn't
tell a handful of alfalfa from oat straw
and who probably never climbed a silo.

I couldn't decide if I felt lucky or not.
What I really wanted to tell you, I said,
was how we used to play on the oat binder
at the back of the machine shed and that
the light fell into place, like ripened oats.
What I really wanted to tell you was that
the oat binder was as beautiful as
a ship under sail, that it took its sweet
time with the field and left all of the gold
for us. What I really wanted to say
is that I know (yes) how lucky I've been.

In Autumn

What affection I have for the earth,
for the meadow already gone to golden,

for the burnt-orange reeds of the cattails,
and the maple leaves etched in yellow

against a pale blue sky, and the black trunk,
and the black branches, and the small black twigs.

In the morning, I remember how much
I love the colors of the sky before

the sun rises, not any one day
the same, changed by the haze in the valley,

the ridges of clouds riding high and white.
In the evening I return—as the light

is caught on the horizon—a glow
of opulence through the soldiering corn.

"H"

Of all tractors, I love the "H" the best:
first for its proportions, the ratio of body to machine,
arm to wheel, leg to clutch, hand to throttle,

and for the way it does not drown the voice,
but forces it to rise above the engine,
and for the smoke signaling from the silver pipe,

for the rip-rap of tread on the big tires, driver
perched between them, as on a throne in kingdoms of oats
and corn, scrolling along the meadow's edge,

then sometimes standing still, engine turning the belt
that turned the wheels in the hammer mill
or whirling the gears that divided the oats from the straw.

And "H" for the ache to see my father plowing fields again—
the silhouette of a red tractor and a man, one hand
on the wheel, the other waving free.

Silo Solo

My father climbs into the silo.
He has come, rung by rung,
up the wooden trail that scales
that tall belly of cement.

It's winter, twenty below zero,
he can hear the wind overhead.
The silage beneath his boots
is so frozen it has no smell.

My father takes up a pick-ax
and chops away a layer of silage.
He works neatly, counter-clockwise
under a yellow light,

then lifts the chunks with a pitchfork
and throws them down the chute.
They break as they fall
and rattle far below.

His breath comes out in clouds,
his fingers begin to ache, but
he skims off another layer
where the frost is forming

and begins to sing, "You are my
sunshine, my only sunshine."

What Every Girl Wants

I wanted a horse. This was long after
we sold the work horses, and I was feeling

restless on the farm. I got up early
to help my father milk the cows, talking

a blue streak about TV cowboys
he never had time to see and trying to

convince him that a horse wouldn't cost
so much and that I'd do all the work.

He listened while he leaned his head
against the flank of a Holstein, pulling

the last line of warm milk into
the stainless bucket. He kept listening

while the milk-machine pumped like an engine,
and the black and silver cups fell off and

dangled down, clanging like bells when he
stepped away, balancing the heavy milker

against the vacuum hose and the leather belt.
I knew he didn't want the trouble

of a horse, but I also knew there was nothing
else I wanted the way I wanted a horse—

another way of saying I wanted
to ride into the sunset and (maybe)

never come back—I think he knew that too.
We'll see, he said, we'll see what we can do.

Watching My Father Shave

I see my father's face in the mirror,
stripping off the white mask that wraps
along his cheekbone, over his mouth,
and, chin jutted up, down his neck.

The silver razor tap-taps the sink;
the ivory-handled brush swishes back
and forth in the cup, and every time
he turns the handle, the faucet squeaks.

I watch the steaming water fill the sink,
and when he splashes it on his face,
the mask dissolves into his waiting hands;
the towel turns on the wooden roller.

How I regret being a girl and never
being able to find myself this way,
to prove how steady I am,
how close to the edge I can come.

Grounded

My father will not
climb into the trees
today.

He is eighty-four
and tells me
that he was never

fond of heights,
that he hated
putting up the pipes

to fill the silo,
that he did not enjoy
climbing to the top

of the barn
to fix the pulley
on the hay-sling.

I have no desire
to be in the air,
he says.

And I always thought
he loved walking
the rim of the silo,

waving his hat
in circles overhead,
shouting down to

where we stood
grounded and gazing
up at him.

July Mirage

He looks up.
For a moment he thought he saw

horses and the hay mower
in the field next to the gravel pit.

More than half a century—
gone the harnesses and the twitching skin

under the reins, gone the quiet way
the hay fell behind the sickle's arm.

He wants to climb onto that rack again,
lift a pitchfork and pull the hay

down, as if it was a river of green
falling from the sky,

to be that young again.

◈

After a certain age, the more one becomes
oneself, the more obvious one's family traits
become.

—Marcel Proust

When You Were Small

Whatever I can't remember must not be true,
and what you did or said is truer than
words I could've scooped up, water in a sieve.

While you slept, I considered other things,
so when you woke you would not feel as if
you'd been measured and fitted to the page.

I wanted you to grow up straight, not bent
beneath the weight of my gaze,
but (naturally) I never stopped looking,

never stopped noticing how quickly one
of you finished the painting, while the other
one was only starting to sketch the scene.

The First Child
(for Sarah)

It is hard to be the first,
the one who opens the door
between generations, who
swings between the mother
and the father, the one who
must learn to sleep through
the night, alone.

        The oldest one,
the eldest, the one who
has her first birthday first
and her second birthday
first, and first rides a bike,
and first goes off to school
and has her picture taken
a hundred times a day.

The first one makes mistakes
that show the others what
to avoid. She must go down
into the dark underworld
of parental ignorance and come
up with a key that will
release her and her sisters
from the fortress where
the ogres planned to keep them
all their lives.

        She has to be
the first to tell them no, make
them let go. She has to tell them
she isn't going to be a virtuoso,
doesn't want straight A's, won't
take accelerated math, has to
find her own way. First to say
love me for who I am.

First to want the car keys, first
to hit a tree, first to stay out
late, first not to come home
at all. She makes them pace
the floor, believing in the aliens
that take the real child and leave
heavy metal in her place.

                         But she's
the first to come back home,
first to remember your birthday
and Mother's Day, a bit
extravagant, as first-borns
tend to be. She begins
to admire the way you arrange
your furniture, pages through
your books, notices the
colors in your kitchen—
and then one day she invites you
to dinner, and clearly
she has spent the whole day
making sure everything
is absolutely
perfect.

Ultrasound

The ultrasound lets us know
the baby is a boy and that
there's only one of him in there.

All four chambers of his heart are
working, and his heart is beating
a hundred-forty-five times a minute.

He's in the uterus, where he
should be and not in a narrow
fallopian tube;

the placenta has moved back
from the cervix (that's good!)
and all his fluid levels

check out just fine. His spine
is nicely formed; his head
and neck proportionate.

No problem with his kidneys (both
present and accounted for); his
tummy's round (a little "chubby")

and from some angles his profile
is clear: the forehead
and a little nose.

The most astonishing (and unusual)
thing is seeing his hands
as they open and close,

as if he's counting all the stars
in heaven, or practicing the art
of letting go.

Waiting for Alicia

Sitting outside
your house,
I hear the dog
you do not have
barking, which is
probably why I
walked around back

to pick an apple
from the tree that is
not there. I also noticed
the vegetable garden
and all of its
nonexistent peas

and carrots, as well as
the usual imaginary rows
of sweet corn and potatoes.
You have such
talent for doing
what can't be done.

Overhead, the sky
was real except for
the hot air balloon
you pretend to keep
on call, and I love
the lake that suddenly

appeared at the end
of your driveway when
all the other houses
disappeared, and now I
wonder how many sails
your ship will have
when you come
gliding into port.

Excavation in D

He's down in the gravel pit all summer,
taking the family apart, layer
by layer, as if it wasn't any

of us who dumped things, but rather some
extravagant beings he never knew.
He's hoping to find a buried treasure—

meanwhile he's assembling wasted pieces
of the past.   Item: stag-handled pocket
knife, "in good condition," he says. "The tip

is broken," says my father. "But the handle's
good and the blade isn't even rusted."
"Still, it hasn't any tip," my father

says, "and I'd throw it away again
if you let me." This goes on all summer.

The Imaginary Photo Album

The photographs I have taken of you,
one shutter at a time, are scattered now

from one house to another. I meant to
put them all in books and write down how

old you were when we went to Yellowstone
and the names you had for the little bear

we bought when you were scared to be alone.
I'm worried that no one will recognize where

you were standing in this one; they won't see
the yard of our first house or recognize

your father's father as he is pushing
his reading glasses up to watch your face

as you open the present they have brought—
that look of happiness the camera caught.

When You Were One

We had to keep you under constant surveillance.
If we looked away for even a minute
you might be pulling down the Christmas tree

or eating the cat's food. You liked anything
small and dusty, and you could spot a crumb
across a large room. Your crawling speed accelerated.

Already at one, you had learned there were
voices inside of the curved thing we held up to
our ears and that closing the door didn't mean

the rest of the world had disappeared.
You were learning hundreds of words,
letting them roll around in the spaces between

the hunks of familiar color and shape
that wrapped around you in the light,
and sometimes I thought I saw a faint glow

beneath the fuzzy hair on your skull—the flash
of neurons. At one, you had a sense of humor
and didn't mind acting surprised at peek-a-boo,

but your attention span was short. If you could
hold it in your hand, you held it for a second or two
and then pitched it straight ahead, full force!

I was hoping to interest you in books, art,
and ancient civilizations, but it appeared
you might want to play some baseball on the side.

When you went to sleep you listened to classical music
on your special CD and held onto your blue blanket.
You weren't afraid of the dark—or anything else.

Your First Baseball Season

There was a lot of rain. I could tell
that you understood its soft sway.

You moved around the diamond like a firefly.
Once you were the catcher, and the next time
I saw you on third base, leaning towards home.

The uniform you wore was long and loose,
but I could almost see you growing into it,
like a second skin.

The night when you turned six, you held
the smallest present in your hands,
closed your eyes for a moment,

and then opened them, the way a batter
does just before he steps into the box.

In This Photo

My mother is reading gravestones. The wind
is ruffling through her red-gold hair, her coat

is blowing in the English air. We'll stay
in Lyme-Regis tonight; we'll walk the Cob

and drink Thomas Hardy ale in the pub.
To my mother, Dorchester is simply

a market town, and she's in the market
for small souvenirs—useful household things

to bring back, wrapped between layers of socks
and sweaters, a memento of this trip we took

when old names in a churchyard reminded
us of everyone we'd ever lost

or left behind, even though we turned to smile
at the camera in my daughter's hand.

My Brother's Hat

And sometimes I am my brother
as I lift my chin to signal "No"
the way he learned to do in Turkey,

and sometimes when I slip my foot
into a shoe I think of the
red scorpions in the jungle

and of the giant rats under the cot
that kept falling apart in Paraguay
and of the piranhas.

And sometimes I dream in Spanish
or Guarani, but never in French because
I know enough to know better,

and I do not buy anything except for
parsley and scallions and other
things I need to make tabouli,

and also the ingredients
for the most delicious (and healthy)
cookies in the world,

and I am he in how I remember
another side of the story, the one
that I never tell, the part

I couldn't see, and, circling the lake,
wondering about the hawk
who dove down and took his hat,

I am he (days later) when it appears
in the branches of a tree, and there
I am, looking up at my hat.

These Few Precepts
                (for Marna)

I said to her, don't leave your life
scattered in boxes across the country,

don't slip away without tying down
the hatch, don't walk a mile out of

your way to avoid a crack, don't
worry about breaking your mother's

back. I'm sorry, I said, that I was
stupid when I married; I'm sorry I

chose for right instead of love, for
truth instead of beauty. They aren't

always the same thing you know,
despite what Keats said. Don't try

to do it all alone, and if you fail,
think of how well you've failed

and how all you really need is a good
view of the sky or a bit of something

—a flower petal or speckled stone—
held close enough for the eye to

drink it in, and remember, I said,
I'll always love you, no matter what.

In Vermeer's Painting
(For Alicia)

In Vermeer's painting she turns
towards us, her head wrapped
in a blue and gold silk turban.
I know those eyes, the nose,

even the lips, parted with her
tongue light on the teeth,
the faint eyebrows, the shadow
and slope of the cheek, the chin.

Of course I'm amazed: what is
my daughter, now standing beside me,
doing in seventeenth century Holland?
von Zutphen, I presume?

She looks pensive, as if the
pearl, floating above her robe
and collar, was indeed the pearl
of wisdom, but I know that

she is thinking about the future
when she will be born in
Lindbergh's town and how someday
she will dance on the moon.

She sees the centuries of pearl
the slow layering of generation
until this particular luster is
reached and stands now

in the museum, tilting her head
(first this way and then that)
to see what she's become:
in Vermeer's painting she turns.

Grandson

When I pick him up at his day care place,
he's been asleep, and is, as his mother

said he would be, sweaty, a bit dazed.
I bring the car seat out to my car while

his daycare mom helps him with his shoes
and jacket. His face is clear,

smooth as a leaf of grass. His eyes
are half-moon slices of blue sky.

When I drive, he doesn't talk, and I can't
tell if that's because he doesn't want to

distract me from the road or if he can't
think of anything amusing to say.

I watch him in the rearview mirror,
and sometimes he smiles and waves.

Miguel and Dan in Mexico

They are standing in the square
listening to a mariachi band—
they are eating pastries, drinking milk.

One of them has a bunch of cameras
around his neck, backpack over his shoulder—
the other has a paper in his hand.

He looks one way, then the other,
and gives a signal as they head out
of San Miguel de Allende.

They did not eat in the courtyard, where
they might have had wine and paella
for less than a Junior Whopper.

They did not stay in the old hotel
on the square, which, it turns out, is cheaper
than the Motel 6 in Freeport, Minnesota,

and when they saw the admission charge,
they did not see the Museum of the Arts.
I know these guys: wherever they go,
they know how it feels to live there.

I Look at You and Wonder
                    (for Sarah)

How did you learn those things
you've always seemed
to know? How did you

know what you wanted
so early, so clearly,
without any

advice from your mystified
mother, who thought
she only wanted

happiness for you?
How did you discover
the hidden agendas,

the secret plans? And where
did you learn to smile
like that

from the inside out
and how to close
a deal

on your own terms,
to tell some guy
to go to hell!

How do you always know
exactly when you're
needed, to fly

through the night and arrive
at the place where you
were born so that

you could brush your grandmother's hair
and say, "It's alright, Gammer.
You can go now."

Happiness

This was when my daughters were just children
playing on the rocky shore of the lake,

their hair in braids, their bright-colored jackets
tied around their waists. It was afternoon,

the shadows falling away, their faces
glowing with light. Whatever we said then

(and it must have been happy; it must have
been hopeful) is lost as I am now lost

from that life I lived. This was when nothing
that I wanted mattered, though all I wanted

was happiness, pure happiness, simple
as strawberries and cream in a saucer,

as curtains floating from a window sill,
as small pairs of shoes arranged in a row.

11:11 (Make a Wish)
(for Marna)

What did you wish?

I wished what I always wish
and that's something
that begins with you
and ends happy.

It starts there
and goes on to
everything.

I believe that one
of the good things
about love
is that it never
needs more than
one wish.

What did you wish?

It was less like seeing than like being for the first time seen, knocked breathless by a powerful glance. The flood of fire abated, but I'm still spending the power.

—Annie Dillard

Things You Didn't Put On Your Resumé

How often you got up in the middle of the night
when one of your children had a bad dream,

and sometimes you woke because you thought
you heard a cry but they were all sleeping,

so you stood in the moonlight just listening
to their breathing, and you didn't mention

that you were an expert at putting toothpaste
on tiny toothbrushes and bending down to wiggle

the toothbrush ten times on each tooth while
you sang the words to songs from *Annie*, and

who would suspect that you know the fingerings
to the songs in the first four books of the Suzuki

Violin Method and that you can do the voices
of Pooh and Piglet especially well, though

your absolute favorite thing to read out loud is
Bedtime for Frances and that you picked

up your way of reading it from Glynnis Johns,
and it is, now that you think of it, rather impressive

that you read all of Narnia and all of the Ring Trilogy
(and others too many to mention here) to them

before they went to bed and on the way out to
Yellowstone, which is another thing you don't put

on the resumé: how you took them to the ocean
and the mountains and brought them safely home.

How We Live

Start with something easy: the fan, blowing
air across the room on a hot day,

ice cubes collapsing in the glass, making
a sound like bells or wooden marimbas.

Add voices on the phone, the radio
in the background (another suicide

bombing), the distant sky between the trees.
Wildfires on the horizon. Add time.

What you wanted was no less than the truth,
something you could hold lightly in your hand.

What you found was this uncertainty,
memory mixed with desire. How we live.

How to Listen

Tilt your head slightly to one side and lift
your eyebrows expectantly. Ask questions.

Delve into the subject at hand or let
things come randomly. Don't expect answers.

Forget everything you've ever done.
Make no comparisons. Simply listen.

Listen with your eyes, as if the story
you are hearing is happening right now.

Listen without blinking, as if a move
might frighten the truth away forever.

Don't attempt to copy anything down.
Don't bring a camera or a recorder.

This is your chance to listen carefully.
Your whole life might depend on what you hear.

November, 1967

Dr. Zhivago was playing at the Paramount
Theater in St. Cloud. That afternoon,
we went into Russia,

and when we came out, the snow
was falling—the same snow
that fell in Moscow.

The sky had turned black velvet.
We'd been through the Revolution
and the frozen winters.

In the Chevy, we waited for the heater
to melt ice on the windshield,
clapping our hands to keep warm.

On the highway, these two things:
a song from *Sgt. Pepper's Lonely Hearts Club Band*
and that semi-truck careening by.

Now I travel through the dark without you
and sometimes I turn up the radio, hopeful
the way you were, no matter what.

The Room

There is always a door,
some way of coming in
leading to a way out.

Usually there is a window
looking out on broken streets
or meadows filled with flowers.

The sun is pouring in,
or the shades are drawn.
You decide.

Inside the room it's quiet,
or the radio blares.
Yes, that's up to you as well.

There is only one chair and a table.
There are couches and paintings.
The room could be empty.

You write in a blue notebook,
or you read far into the night
You sit and dream.

You have known so many rooms,
so many ways of looking out a window,
ways of going in and out the door.

When will you grow weary of doors
and windows? of walls and ceilings?
Yes, that's also for you to decide.

In the Photo Booth

I leaned forward to put my quarters
into the slot. The directions said Hold Still.
Look Straight Ahead. Smile. (I did not.) Soon

a strip of faces fell out of the wall—
all mine, one after another, and none of them
what I wanted. That was back when my eyes

were green; that was back when my hair was still
dark. I needed one of those photos—it
didn't matter which—for a rail pass that

would last all spring. And the rest of the strip?
I threw it away. Too bad! I could use
that face—that earnest young face—today.

Thinking Back

If I think back, the house
we live in now goes
back to belonging
to someone else. Paint
comes off of the walls
and swirls its color
back to white. Paintings
lose their frames
and lean on the easel,
wet and unfinished.
The bed is unmade, and
all that love is waiting.

If I think back, words
get unsaid, and ink
disappears from the page.
None of us has ever
tasted sushi, no one
has left the continent, and
there are stories we have
never read together.

Back much farther
and we have no children,
and even farther back
we're in a clearing
about to fill with oak trees
before we return to the edge
of a lake, before we go back
to crossing oceans from
a place too far back to see.

School Movies

Once a year, around Christmas,
we'd get to see the only movie
the grade school owned.

Sitting in rows of wooden chairs
on the basketball court, we'd pretend
we loved *The Miracle of Our Lady of Fatima*

when really we wished that all three
children would meet Count Dracula
on the mountainside instead of

the Blessed Virgin Mary. Mary, we knew,
would make them into saints, would
make the skeptical villagers

believe in miracles. For years we hoped
for something different, and then
finally, it came—

first, *The Yearling*, dying in the boy's arms;
then *Old Yeller*, foaming at the mouth,
nothing to do but shoot him,

and then the voice of *Nature*, describing the rattlesnake
lying in wait for the prairie dog, the lion
descending on the wildebeest.

The Toaster

I thought of it in London
when the rain was falling

in that syncopated, multi-
tudinous way the rain likes

to fall on the century's
pavements and courtyards.

I could see so clearly its
patterned back and worn black

knobs. I could smell the
crumbs burning on the coils

that glowed red when the great
silver wings were opened wide.

It was as beautiful as anything
they keep in the V&A, but I

imagined it now—layered in rock
and root in the gravel pit—its

frayed diamond cord looking just
like an occasional garter snake.

On the Way to the Farm I Think of My Sister

There's a different highway now
coming across different fields
west of the old double lane.

Once you're on it, you don't have to stop
for anything, except congestion in July
when everyone else is heading

North. You'd like it: driving at 80 mph
with the music forty years past when
you left the planet . . . but no more

gasoline at 29 cents a gallon! No more
Beatles (John and George— both dead),

no more cows in the stanchions, no more hay
in the barn. Otherwise, everything is
pretty much the way you remember it.

The Shadow

Then again, it could have been a lampshade,
or a vase of wheat or a stack of books.

It could have been the statue of a god
or the reflection of an owl across

the fields, but then again it could have been
exactly what it seemed to be: someone

sitting at a desk, looking out but not
at me, someone's legendary head, though

I suppose it could have been illusion,
a floating face, imagination's trick;

I suppose it could have been that backward
glance in time, the one we talked about this

morning at breakfast—some other then that
rhymes with now and then never goes away.

Myth

First it was months
and then years; they went by
so slowly at first

and then everything picked up
speed. I suppose you could say
we forgot you—it's true

that after a while I stopped
wondering what you would
have said about the men

I met and the new songs on
the radio. I learned how
to make my own choices.

What else could I do? You
went down into the earth
as surely as Persephone

and we were not gods that
we could make the earth
yield you up again, though

lately I dream
there is a very simple answer
that I once thought I knew.

The Lost Day

How can memory be so fickle?
How can it be so stubborn?

Why is the bad child of the brain
in charge of its treasures?

Who cares whether reason can make its argument?
Who worries whether imagination will fail?

But why can't memory
go into the rooms of the past

and bring back that one day we ask for—
the only one we want,

the one we placed there so carefully
saving it for now

when we would (at last)
sit down and listen

when we would give it
our undivided attention

when we would love it
for what it was.

Snow at the Farm

My father gets his tractor out.
It is winter, finally—the first
big snow of the year—and

he is eighty-four. He does not leap
into the seat the way that I
remember, but once he's there

he pulls down the brim of his cap,
and all-in-one his legs and arms
work at clutches, throttles, and

levers as he pushes and loads
the snow into neat hills at
the edge of the yard. The sun

is a bright shield in the sky,
something I cannot bear to look at,
and the snow is so white that

it shows black where the plow
cuts in. From the kitchen window
I watch the red tractor moving

back and forth through the blue
and white world, my father's
hands at the wheel.

The Last Things I'll Remember

The partly open hay barn door, white frame around the darkness,
the broken board, small enough for a child
to slip through.

Walking in the cornfields in late July, green tassels overhead,
the slap of flat leaves as we pass, silent
and invisible from any road.

Hollyhocks leaning against the stucco house, peonies heavy
as fruit, drooping their deep heads
on the dog house roof.

Lilac bushes between the lawn and the woods,
a tractor shifting from one gear into
the next, the throttle opened,

the smell of cut hay, rain coming across the river,
the drone of the hammer mill,
milk machines at dawn.

Like a Diamond

In your sky, the stars
are made of many colors.

No outlines of legendary lovers,
the ache of their almost touching

arching through the dark.
Your stars are all equal

and fill the purple-blue expanse
without a sound. You could

give them names and match
each one with a song. I'd help

if you asked me—I could begin
saying the words right now.

Acknowledgments

"The Kingdom of Summer," *Prairie Home Companion Show*, 1998.

"Bringing in the Hay," *Minnesota Poetry Calendar*, 2001.

"The First Child," *Dust and Fire*, 2001.

"These Few Precepts, *Dust and Fire*, 2001.

"Watching My Father Shave," *Passages Northwest*, 2002.

"The Body I Once Lived In," *The Wolf*, 2003

"Thinking Back," *Water~Stone Review*, 2004.

"Myth," *Sidewalks Online*, 2005.

"Asking My Father About the Horses," *Great River Review*, 2005.

"In the Family" *Great River Review*, 2005.

"School Movies," *We Are What We Watch: Poets Respond to Movies, TV, and Media*, 2006.

"My Brother's Hat," *The Wolf*, 2005.

"Harrow," Minnesota Artists Online, 2006.

"Things You Didn't Put on Your Resumé," *The Writer's Almanac*, 2006.

"What Every Girl Wants," *The Blueroad Reader, Stardust and Fate*, 2007

"H," *Knockout*, 2009.

"Breakfast," "Zucchini Bread," *Turtle Literary Magazine*, 2009.

"Picking Rocks," *Green Blade*, 2009.

"The Last Things I'll Remember," *Great River Review*, 2009.

"The Oat Binder," *Water~Stone Review*, Fall, 2009.

Joyce Sutphen grew up on a farm near St. Joseph, Minnesota and currently lives in Chaska, Minnesota. She has degrees from the University of Minnesota, including a Ph.D. in Renaissance Drama. Her first book, *Straight Out of View*, won the Barnard New Women's Poets Prize (Beacon Press, 1995, republished by Holy Cow! Press in 2001). *Coming Back to the Body* (Holy Cow! Press, 2000) was a finalist for a Minnesota Book Award, and *Naming the Stars* (Holy Cow! Press 2004), won a Minnesota Book Award in Poetry. In 2005, Red Dragonfly Press published *Fourteen Sonnets* in a letter-press edition, and in 2006 Sutphen co-edited the award-winning anthology *To Sing Along the Way: Minnesota Women Poets from the Territorial Days to the Present* (New Rivers Press). Her poems have appeared in *Poetry*, *American Poetry Review*, *Atlanta Review*, *Minnesota Monthly*, *North Dakota Review*, and many other journals, and she has been a guest on *A Prairie Home Companion*, hosted by Garrison Keillor.